CONTENTS

HIGHLY INFLUENTIAL

Rap and hip-hop are closely related musical **genres** created in the early 1970s. At first, small pockets of fans appeared in East Coast cities, but in just one decade, you could find rap and hip-hop fans from coast to coast! Today rap and hip-hop are two of the most popular musical forms around the world. Both musical genres have had a significant **influence** on other genres, including rock, pop, and even country music.

In many ways, rap and hip-hop are the result of people feeling **marginalized** in American society. Its roots are based in Black and Hispanic communities that struggled to be heard, recognized, and respected.

Art All Around Us

HIP-HOP AND RAP

Ezra E. Knopp

CREATED BY Humans

Published in 2026 by The Rosen Publishing Group, Inc.
2544 Clinton Street, Buffalo, NY 14224

First Edition

Editor: Greg Roza
Designer: Michael Flynn

Photo Credits: Cover DC Studio/Shutterstock.com; (series background) Yuliya Chsherbakova/Shutterstock.com; pp. 5, 13 lev radin/Shutterstock.com; p. 7 Alessandro Lucca/Shutterstock.com; p. 9 https://commons.wikimedia.org/wiki/File:Herc_on_the_Wheels_of_Steel.JPG; p. 11 spatuletail/Shutterstock.com; p. 14 Franklin Sheard Jr/Shutterstock.com; p. 15 (top) Adam McCullough/Shutterstock.com; p. 15 (bottom) Nikola Spasenoski/Shutterstock.com; p. 17 Kraft74/Shutterstock.com; p. 18 Jamie Lamor Thompson/Shutterstock.com; p. 19 Adam McCullough/Shutterstock.com; p. 20 (left) https://commons.wikimedia.org/wiki/File:Salt-n-Pepa_2013.jpg; p. 20 (right) Featureflash Photo Agency/Shutterstock.com; p. 21 (top left) admedia/Shutterstock.com; p. 21 (top right) A.PAES/Shutterstock.com; p. 21 (bottom) Jgphotographydetroit/Shutterstock.com; p. 23 1000 Words/Shutterstock.com; p. 25 https://commons.wikimedia.org/wiki/File:TR-808_-_MIM,_Phoenix_(2019-08-30_14.59.26_by_Bryan_Pocius)_(cropped).jpg; p. 26 (left) L Paul Mann/Shutterstock.com; p. 27 (right) Kathy Hutchins/Shutterstock.com; p. 27 (main) Kevin RC Wilson/Shutterstock.com; p. 27 (inset) Joe Seer/Shutterstock.com; p. 29 AnnaStills/Shutterstock.com.

Cataloging-in-Publication Data
Names: Knopp, Ezra E.
Title: Hip-hop and rap / Ezra E. Knopp.
Description: Buffalo, NY : Created by Humans, an imprint of Rosen Publishing, 2026. | Series: Art all around us | Includes glossary and index.
Identifiers: ISBN 9781534552814 (pbk.) | ISBN 9781534552821 (library bound) | ISBN 9781534552838 (ebook)
Subjects: LCSH: Rap (Music)--History and criticism--Juvenile literature. | Hip-hop--History--Juvenile literature. | Rap (Music)--Social aspects--Juvenile literature.
Classification: LCC ML3531.K655 2026 | DDC 781.649--dc23

Manufactured in the United States of America

CPSIA Compliance Information: Batch #CWCBH26. For Further Information contact Rosen Publishing at 1-800-237-9932.

Cardi B, shown here, has been called the "Reigning Queen of Hip-Hop" by numerous publications.

WHAT'S THE DIFFERENCE?

Rap is a genre of music that focuses mainly on rhythmic, rhyming lyrics over drum beats and instrumental music. Rap might be thought of as poetry spoken to rhythms and repeated musical patterns. Many rap artists use prerecorded music, often called loops, and electronic drum beats with their songs. Other rap bands use live instruments.

Hip-hop music often includes rapping, but it's also thought of as a cultural movement. Compared to rap, hip-hop includes more instruments. Typical themes in both rap and hip-hop include personal struggles and successes, social **commentary**, and political issues.

Both hip-hop and rap were created in 1973 in the Bronx, New York. Early artists were influenced by funk, soul, and disco music, as well as African traditions of storytelling.

OLD SCHOOL ORIGINS

Hip-hop's origins come from soul and funk music. Disco was very popular at the time, and some funk bands began to **parody** the genre. These early efforts led to the rise of hip-hop.

In 1973, Bronx native Clive Campbell, better known as DJ Kool Herc, hosted a back-to-school party with his sister. Herc was known to play records from his father's collection while talking over the musical parts. People liked to dance to these parts as well. Herc linked two turntables (record players) each playing the same record, so the musical sections repeated, leaving more time for rapping and dancing.

DJ Kool Herc was also a graffiti artist and a breakdancer. Many consider him the first hip-hop MC and DJ.

KEY ELEMENTS OF HIP-HOP

MCing: MCing (rapping) is a talent for talking to crowds using rhythm and rhyme. "MC" is short for "master of ceremonies," a term for entertainers who host events, entertain crowds, and introduce other entertainers.

DJing: "DJ" is short for "disc jockey," or someone who plays records for a radio station or club. In the world of hip-hop, it can also mean someone who creates music using turntables and **mixers** to loop together extended songs. This often includes "scratching" or dragging the record back and forth against the needle to make unique sounds.

Breakdancing: This energetic form of dancing originated as routines performed during instrumental breaks in songs. Breakdancing was featured in the 2024 Olympic Games!

Graffiti: Before the rise of hip-hop, graffiti was common in New York City. It was used to "tag" or mark gang territory, but has become a colorful and important form of modern art.

The fifth key element of hip-hop is knowledge, or understanding the genre's history and influence on society.

INTO THE GOLDEN AGE

DJ Kool Herc inspired others. Afrika Bambaataa was an early DJ and rapper to come out of the new movement. Grandmaster Flash is credited with mastering DJ scratching techniques. Like Herc, both artists are from the Bronx.

The first hip-hop song to gain widespread success was released in 1979—Sugarhill Gang's "Rapper's Delight." Grandmaster Flash and the Furious Five signed with record company Sugar Hill Records in 1980. They gained widespread success with their 1982 album *The Message*.

Run-DMC led rap artists into the golden age of hip-hop. In 1987, *King of Rock* became the first rap album to **go platinum**.

In the United States, *YO! MTV Raps* aired on cable music channel MTV from 1988 until 1995. It introduced young viewers to many hip-hop and rap artists. The show's first host, Fab Five Freddy, is a famous graffiti artist.

EAST VS. WEST VS. SOUTH

Although hip-hop was an East Coast creation, it didn't take long to spread across the country. Rappers are sometimes sorted into regions. These groups haven't always got along, each arguing that their form of rap is best. The following performers are standouts for each region.

EAST

- The Notorious B.I.G.
- Nas
- 50 Cent
- Lil' Kim
- Wu-Tang Clan

50 Cent

WEST

- Ice Cube
- Tupak Shakur
- Yo-Yo
- Snoop Dog
- Dr. Dre

Snoop Dog

SOUTH

- Outkast
- Lil Wayne
- T.I.
- Ludacris
- Missy Elliott

Missy Elliott

The Midwest has also produced some of hip-hop's greatest artists, including Eminem, Da Brat, and Common.

DANGEROUS MUSIC?

Tupac Shakur is widely considered one of rap's most influential artists. He spoke about the problems Black males face. Shakur had been arrested several times for shooting people. Shakur himself had also been shot several times. In 1996, Shakur was shot by someone in a passing car; he died soon after. This event and others like it made many people label rap and hip-hop "violent" or "dangerous" music.

However, it's unfair to say that rap and hip-hop are **inherently** violent music genres. As many people have pointed out, rap and hip-hop music often reflects the environment in which artists grew up. Today, most people remember Shakur as a poet and a **prophet**, and not a gangster.

While many rap artists address violent issues, some listeners don't recognize the political and social commentary they're conveying. Shakur's music is respected today because of its colorful storytelling and because it shines a light on the problems marginalized groups of people face.

AROUND THE WORLD

Rap and hip-hop have had a huge influence on other musical genres, but also on political movements, social movements, and artistic forms other than music. Many hip-hop artists—such as Queen Latifah, Tupak Shakur, Ice-T, and Ice Cube, to name just a few—launched successful acting careers in addition to music careers. Today, rap artists from countries around the world have used hip-hop and rap to create innovative music.

Ice Cube

In 2018, Kendrick Lamar won the **Pulitzer Prize** for Music. He's the only musical artist outside the genres of classical music and jazz to win the award. This showed the world that hip-hop is a **legitimate** and truly important artform.

Latino Influence

Many Latino artists have helped shaped rap and hip-hop. Cypress Hill released their first album in 1989. Their members have Cuban and Mexican backgrounds. Cypress Hill's unique musical style has influenced many other artists. Other influential Latino hip-hop artists include Pitbull, Bad Bunny, Cardi B, and Daddy Yankee.

GROUNDBREAKING ALBUMS

These albums are just a few hip-hop classics. Have you heard them?

Salt-N-Pepa
Hot, Cool, & Vicious

Run-DMC
King of Rock

Public Enemy
It Takes a Nation of Millions to Hold Us Back

Lauryn Hill
The Miseducation of Lauryn Hill

Eminem
The Marshall Mathers LP

LET'S RAP!

How can you express your thoughts through rap music? What themes interest you most? The best way to find out is to get pen and paper and start crafting your own rap lyrics! At first you may need to list some ideas you care about. Then it's time to add rhyme, rhythm, and creative expression to your work.

Not everyone is comfortable being in front of a crowd. To break away from stage fright, you may start by sharing your lyrics with people close to you to get some **feedback**. In addition to songwriting, it can help to learn an instrument such as keyboards or drums.

Aspiring DJs may have a harder time getting the tools they need. Microphones, turntables, and mixers can cost a lot of money. However, you can usually rent the equipment or even borrow them.

DJ TECHNOLOGY

Music technology has had a great influence on hip-hop and rap, especially for DJs.

turntables: DJs use turntables to play music and create rhythmic scratching sounds.

mixers: Also called mixing boards, mixers combine signals from microphones, turntables, computers, and instruments and produce a balanced sound. DJs create unique music on the fly with the variety of dials and switches on a mixer.

samplers: Samplers, sometimes part of a **synthesizer**, record bits of audio (or samples). DJs save the audio as digital files and can replay them later. Today, sampling is often done with software on computers.

drum machines: Drum machines are electronic musical instruments that produce drum sounds. DJs can create beats and save them for future use.

The TR-808 was an affordable drum machine popular with hip-hop artists in the 1980s. It's particularly valued for its rich, deep, bass drum sound.

HIP-HOP SUPERSTARS

Rap and hip-hop artists are some of the biggest superstars in the world today. Here are a few currently at the top of their game . . . and the music charts!

Kendrick Lamar

Tyler, the Creator

Cardi B

Megan Thee Stallion

THE RAP ARTIST IN YOU

The artists, groups, and albums discussed in this book are just the surface of a vast ocean of hip-hop music. There are many more artists to discover! Also, hip-hop has affected other forms of art today, including street art and fine art, film and television, dance, and much more.

If you were to write rap lyrics, what would you choose to write about? Start with simple topics you know a lot about. This could be your family and friends, your hobbies, or even your favorite foods. Practice your writing, rhyming, and rapping styles. Then, you can move on to other topics, such as social commentary and political discussion.

You don't really need all of the DJ equipment shown here to get started writing rap lyrics. You can always add drum beats or instrumentation later.

GLOSSARY

commentary: A series of explanations or opinions about a main topic, such as society.

feedback: Helpful information that someone gives to show what can be improved.

genre: A particular type or category of literary, musical, or artistic creation, such as hip-hop music or science-fiction writing.

go platinum: In the recording business, to sell more than one million copies of an album.

influence: An effect one thing has on another.

inherent: Belonging to or being a part of the nature of a person or thing.

legitimate: Genuinely good, impressive, or capable of success.

marginalized: Placed in a position of little or no importance, influence, or power.

mixer: An electronic device that combines several elements (voice, music, samples, etc.) to create a balanced song.

parody: A written or musical work in which the style of an author or work is imitated for comic effect.

prophet: One who foretells future events.

Pulitzer Prize: Any of various annual prizes (as for outstanding literary or journalistic achievement) established by the will of newspaper publisher Joseph Pulitzer.

synthesizer: A computer-controlled keyboard that creates and modifies sound.

FOR MORE INFORMATION

BOOKS

Chang, Jeff, and Dave Cook. *Can't Stop Won't Stop: A Hip-Hop History.* New York, NY: Wednesday Books, 2021.

Morall-Baker, Monica B. *The Beat of a Nation: How Hip-Hop Shaped American Culture and Inspired the World.* Minneapolis, MN: Lerner Publications, 2026.

WEBSITES

DJ Kool Herc: Father of Hip Hop
www.djkoolherc.com/copy-of-bio
Read more about DJ Kool Herc at his official website.

Kendrick Lamar
www.biography.com/musicians/kendrick-lamar
Read about the life of Kendrick Lamar and find links to other influential hip-hop artists.

INDEX